God Is Rearranging Your Destiny

by Debra A. Bennett

DebraBennettMinistry@gmail.com

PITTSBURGH, PENNSYLVANIA 15238

RoseDog Books
585 Alpha Drive
Suite 103
Pittsburgh, PA 15238
Visit our website at *www.rosedogbookstore.com*

ISBN: 979-8-88729-290-8
eISBN: 979-8-88729-790-3

Table of Contents

Introduction

This book is inspired by the Holy Spirit, and written according to biblical principals. It's written for those who have questions that God is going to answer. If you are reading this book, God is calling you into action to take your rightful place as a disciple in the body of Christ. He is commissioning you despite your human weaknesses and failures.

God chose you because of what He sees in you. He doesn't judge you for what you are; but instead sees how He can transform you, when you surrender to Him.

God wants you to see the world through His eyes, expand your vision, and see the church's needs, including the role you will play in this new millennium. Destiny awaits you. Remember, when you fall or face obstacles beyond your strength, pick up God's power; no weapons formed against you will be able to stop you.

Make sure you are walking in 100% obedience to God, and be willing to lose sight of your plans, dreams, visions, interests, and goals for the Gospel's sake. Be ready to do the will of the Father, knowing He is the one who called you and commissioned you into action for ministry. There is a need for you to go through God's school to prepare yourself to be a surmounter over every obstacle and temptation that occur in your life. Temptation only becomes a snare to you when you willing yield yourself over to it.

Everyone who accepts Christ as their savior has a job to do for the kingdom of God; it may not be in the pulpit. Perhaps your assignment is the way you live for Christ, and it will draw men unto Him. Ask God what role you must play in the Earth Realm concerning the body of Christ. Remember, if Jesus was not exempt from going through trials, you will not be exempt either. Embrace the moment and be receptive to your call of duty.

Chapter 1

Hold On! A Change Is Coming

A change is on the way. It's hard to smile when your world seems to be tumbling down. You have been in a problematic situation for so long that you have become complacent. It won't always be that way; your deliverance is coming. It is nearer than you can imagine. Instead of pretending to be happy with a fake smile, look out! A real one is about to explode. The rainbow in your life is about to have an ending. God wrote the end of your life before the beginning. Trials come in life to make you a conqueror for the next battle you will face. Each time the battle gets easier and easier; don't give up the fight or your faith. It may seem as though God has forgotten your name and what you're going through right now. You're not forgotten. God has His moments where He stays silent and says nothing. It doesn't mean He doesn't care. He's strategizing the next best move for you. And today you're going to a new level with no hindrances.

When God gets ready to bring a change in your life, there is no devil in hell that can hold it back or stop it from coming to pass. Pray that God gives you endurance and staying power until your breakthrough comes. It's on the way. Hold on! He's working things out in your favor, and things are being turned around just for you.

When you refuse to wait on your change to come, you will find yourself in seasons and cycles of being up and down, and you'll never find stability. You take one step forward and two steps backward. Negativity and disbelief keeps you from holding on until your change comes. It moves you to the end of the line. It causes you to give up. Every time you fail a test with God, you must start all over again. This hinders you from holding on to God's unchanging hand.

Positive thinking keeps you moving forward in the right direction. Push out negative thoughts and replace them with pleasant thinking and reading the word of God daily. Try reading the book of Psalms. When David was in despair, he wrote comforting scriptures to combat every circumstance he faced.

While you are holding on, speak to your spirit and let it know you are not taking steps backward anymore. Rebuke negative thoughts that weigh you down. Remember, you can do all things through Christ that strengthens you.

Push through your problems and face them head on with the word of God in your mouth. Speak those things that are not as though they were. Decree and declare what are yours to come in Jesus' name. Don't be afraid to do those things you think you're not good enough to do. Put yourself to the challenge and try it.

Disbelief will cause you to miss God in your due season every time, just as the children of Israel missed God and wandered aimlessly for forty years in the wilderness without entering the promised land He had allotted them. Disbelief will cause you to be in seasons and cycles of taking one step forward and two steps backward and miss the riches God has prepared for you to enjoy.

Don't let disbelief rule you or gain a foothold in your life. It will cause you to be pushed backwards. When the smallest doubt pops up in your mind, thrust it out in Jesus' name. Become vigilant in everything you accomplish, stay on guard, and keep your mind stayed on Jesus.

Chapter 2

While Waiting on God

While waiting on God means you trust Him. In this life you will always be confronted with waiting on something to come to pass, whether it's a prophecy, dream, or a situation to turn around. When it's not happening as fast as you would like it to, it's easy to get discouraged. The moment you pray, God establishes a set time on earth to bring your promise to pass. He has a set time for you to meet the right mate, a time for your healing, promotion, and breakthrough. It may not be tomorrow, next week, next month, or three years from now; you must keep in mind timing is very crucial and important to God. You don't get to map out your destiny.

When you understand that your timing has been ordered by God, it takes the weight off of you. You can relax while you're waiting on God. You can have all the prayer warriors in the world pray for you every day of the year, but God sets your time. All you have to do is sit back and be patient. Wait on His timing for whatever it is you have been believing Him for. He is not going to move any faster than His appointed time. You can't hurry God. Time waiting on God is not time wasted.

When God sets a time for your miracle or breakthrough to occur, there is nothing anyone can do. It is a done deal. It has been approved by God. There is no boy, girl, woman, or man of God who can change God's mind. You can pray fervently day and night, but you are not going to get that job, promotion, house, financial breakthrough, or healing until God's allotted time. Relax! You don't have to worry whether it's going to happen. You must know that the promise has already been established by God. You may have been praying about a situation for a long time, but you don't see anything happening. Just start thanking God in advance because He is working behind the scenes to put everything into motion.

Here is where it takes faith in God. He gives you promises for the future, but He doesn't always tell you when they will occur. When you pray for something, ask God how long you will have to wait, knowing will make the waiting process go by smoothly. He may not give you the answer you want to hear, but are you willing to wait until it comes to pass? Remember this one thing: God's timing is not yours. Therefore, with patience wait on Him.

As busy as Jesus was, He went to the well and waited all day long for one woman. He waited to give her a breakthrough. When you truly believe and take God at His word, you are at peace. "He who has believed enter into rest" (Hebrews 4:3). He who believes knows the answer is on the way. The right people and opportunity are on the way; you are going to come into your set time of favor. There is a set time when the right phone call and favor will hit your household. There is a time and season for everything under the sun. If you are still waiting on your promise to come to pass, that means you haven't given up, even though it looks like the promise will never take place.

God has not forgotten you; your promised spouse is on the way. He is still giving out blessings. There is no one and nothing who can stop it from coming to pass. He sees your hand raised. It's not that He hasn't answered your request. Sometimes there is demonic inference in the atmosphere that tries to stop the flow of your breakthrough. God will send His Holy Angels to clear the way of demonic trafficking like He did for Daniel. His blessings were held up for twenty-one days, but God sent Michael the archangel to clear the way of demonic interference so Daniel could receive the answer to his prayer request.

When God gets ready to bless and deliver you, there is no devil in hell that can hold you back or block your blessings from coming to pass. You are the only one who can block your blessings. Make sure there is no hidden sin in your life, especially holding a grudge against someone in un-forgiveness. Those things are blessing blockers. Trust in the Lord, even when you can't figure out what He's doing, knowing that it will all work together for your good.

Chapter 3

Forget the Past and Move Forward

Don't let your past negatively affect your future. How long will you continue to grieve? What has happened is over; you can't go back and change it. But you can positively put it under the blood of Jesus, so the enemy will not have reasonable assurance to bring accusations against you before the Lord. If you are wondering if your pain will ever go away, yes, it will go away when you realize Jesus paid and made the ultimate sacrifice for your sins of guilt and shame. You don't need drugs or alcohol to relieve or numb your pain. All you need is Jesus and faith in God. Now, get ready! Because God is getting ready to move on your behalf. He is about to blow your mind for the next move in your life.

When the enemy tries to remind you of what you did in your past, remind him of what Jesus did for your future. Rebuke the devil, and he will flee. Stay focused on what God called you to do. Don't allow memories to get in your way. The pain you endured has gotten you to where you are now in Christ Jesus. God chose you; He used your past to affect your future. He knew everything you were going to do before you entered this world, and He still decided to use you.

Stop allowing past dilemmas to affect your destiny! All of it is under the blood of Jesus. God has been protecting you since you were in your mother's womb. Don't let past mistakes become thorns in your flesh. They are the catalyst that will catapult you into your future.

The Apostle Paul in the New Testament talks about the thorn that was in his flesh. His thorn was the memories of the Christians he persecuted before he converted to Christianity. But he didn't let it stop him from reaching the destiny that awaited him. He worked miracles, and souls were saved under his ministry until the day he transitioned into Heaven. His trials were only temporal for him, but he went into eternity that will last him forever and likewise for every believer.

The trials and turmoil you have faced have pushed you to your appointed destiny. Don't quit, and don't stop. God has you in the palm of His hand. Everyone has something in their past that was not pleasing to God, but He looked beyond it and sent His only begotten son, Jesus, to save humanity.

You must push your way through life's obstacles and hold onto your faith in God. Remember, Jesus paid the ultimate price to forgive all your sins with no exceptions.

Chapter 4

You Are Not a Failure Because You Failed

When you are in Christ Jesus, failure is never an option. You're not a failure because you faced many challenges of setbacks and delays. Some failures are of God to let you know you are off course. Perhaps life has thrown you a curve ball. But this is not the end of your story. God has a definite plan for your life; He is rewriting your story. You're being rerouted because you have gotten off course. Your life has been put on a timeline that has been predestined before the foundation of the universe. The Angels in Heaven are opening up your books in Heaven right now as you get on board.

The reason you can't keep a job is because you are where you're not supposed to be. You can't work on a job God didn't ordain for you. When you are in the right place at the right time, things will begin to fall into place for you. Until you ask God what career He wants you to embark upon, you will find yourself switching jobs quite often. If you sincerely ask Him what career He has ordained for you, the open door will be waiting for you. Your will has to be His will. The word of God says, "Thy will be done on earth as it is in heaven." Say it and mean it.

God was protecting you in all your struggles, delays, and setbacks. His hand was invisible behind the scene. He was waiting for a time such as this to grow you into maturity to handle the things of God. You don't need others to validate who you are; God is raising you up. This is the last time you will see failure inside of you. The Holy Spirit resides in you, which makes you more than a conqueror; you are victorious through Christ Jesus. God still has a purpose and plan for your life; you're not a waste, and you're not alone. Don't look at how far someone else has gotten in life. The race is not given to the swift but to the one who endures to the end. There is greatness inside of you. Don't quit, and don't give up. Trust God even when you can't feel Him. He said, "For I know the plans I have for you, plans to prosper you and not to harm you, plans to give you hope and a great expected end" (Jeremiah 29:11).

God knows your thoughts. Keep your mind stayed on Him. He has kept you all this time, and He is not about to let you down now! He has invested too much in you to let you wander aimlessly and fail. You are in the palm of His hand. He has been looking over you since you came out of your mother's womb. When this life has dealt you the worst hand imaginable, look to God and start praising and worshiping Him, and all the pain will fade away.

God is going to surround you with the right people in your life at the right time. He's going to move on your behalf and give you a great expected end. He's preparing the right contacts for you right now. He was with you through all your trials, tribulations, and pain. Now, your past is being erased, and your marital problems and bad relationships are being resolved. The devour is being rebuked for your sake. You're being redirected and put on a definite path of recovery today. No more setbacks and delays. Today is the day of new beginnings in your life.

Chapter 5

God Knows Your Hiding Place

There is no hiding place when you're hurting: It shows up all over your face. God knows where you are. You smile for the world, but you are dying spiritually on the inside. No one knows your hidden place but you and God. You are living in a world where ups and downs seem to be inevitable. You're surrounded by family and friends, but they don't know what's going on inside of you. Yes, life has been rough for you; it has given you disappointment after disappointment with no hope. Now, you are hiding because you want everyone around you to think you have it all together. The truth is, no one has it all together. As a matter of fact, no one knows you don't have it all together but you and God. Things may not have worked out according to plan. Whose plans are you trying to follow, yours or God's? It's not over until God says it's over. He wants you to stop chasing a dream He shut the door to twenty years ago.

Your prideful, arrogant spirit has caused you to be in this place in your life. Trying to make people think you are what you are not has brought calamity to you. When you walk humbly and have a fall in life, no one will know you fell; but when you have been boastful during good times, everyone around you will know when you fall. This is what has caused you to be in a place where no one knows where you are but you and God. I'm talking about that hiding place on the inside of you. The world sees a strong person who has it all together. They don't see what's really going on with you. Your tears are temporary, and they will be relieved. Give up pretending to be someone you are not; it has brought you misery and pain. Become transparent with God, and He will bring you out of your dilemma. You are in a place where you don't know how to come out; don't stay there and nurse your wounds. God is going to take you to a place called "there," everywhere you go He will be there. Whenever Jesus shows up, all of Satan's power is broken.

When Adam and Eve fell from grace and were hiding in the garden, only God knew where they were. When the prophet Elijah hid in the woods, only God knew where Adam and Elijah were, because he called them by name. Now, God is calling you by name for restoration. For it to begin, you must be filled with the knowledge of God's will. Your mind must be continually transformed, changed from selfish thinking, carnal thoughts and renewed by the word of God. As your mind is renewed, the Holy Spirit will fill you with God's will. It will become the driving force behind all your decision making, actions, and motives.

Surrender your hiding place to God today. Let Him heal your brokenness. He has the pieces of your life in His hands. Step-by-step He will bring everything back into alignment again as you become transparent and walk humbly. In doing so, you won't have to face embarrassment, nor will you have to turn around and run for cover when things go wrong in your life.

Come out of your hiding place! God is renewing you right now. He's restoring all your losses and the years the locusts took from you. More than what you had before is coming your way. God is renewing you right now! You can begin right where you are, regardless of your age. God is picking up the broken pieces and putting you back together again. "Trust in the Lord with all your heart and lean not to your own understanding and He will direct your path" (Proverbs 3:5–6, KJV).

Chapter 6

It is God; How to Know His Voice

God is still speaking to His people today, like He is speaking to you right now. He doesn't speak in a loud audible voice like he did with Moses. When Jesus came into the earth realm, He brought in a new dispensation of the Holy Spirit that resides on the inside of you when you accept Christ as your savior. He no longer lives in a box called the Ark of the Covenant. Your body is now the Ark of the New Covenant, where the Holy Spirit resides in you. His voice comes to you in many forms.

He speaks to you through His Spirit, which is your first thought, so you can do that which is pleasing in the sight of God. He speaks through His prophets, ministers, and through people. When you have prayed about something no one knew about except you and God, someone will come along and give you the answer to your prayer unknowingly. He speaks to you through your Bible reading time, dreams, visions, nature, and signs around you. For example, you might be getting ready to make a very important decision about something, and God will show you a stop sign that signals you to stop because you're getting ready to make a big mistake. It is also good to listen to the lyrics in songs. God speaks very loud through music; it is one of the ways He convey messages to you, and you will feel His presence indicating He is speaking directly to you.

One mistake many parents make is dismissing what their children have to say. God often uses them to speak to parents. Therefore, don't dismiss what they say so easily. Hear what they have to say. If you are not sure you heard from God, allow the Holy Spirit to lead you on a fast. Whenever you are led to fast, you will notice something with the word "fast" on it, or you will feel a tugging in your spirit to let you know that the Lord is leading you in that direction.

Allow the Holy Spirit to lead you when taking trips. Pray for traveling grace and protection for yourself, family members, and friends. Ask the Holy Spirit what day and time you should leave. Many incidents, accidents, and deaths have been prevented by praying and being led by the Holy Spirit about when to travel. The word of God said, "Trust in the Lord with all thy heart and soul and lead not to thy own understanding but, in all thy ways acknowledge Him and He shall direct thy paths" (Proverbs 3:5–6 KJV).

Now that you know how to hear God's voice more clearly, start listening when He speaks. Everything you have read and are about to read is God speaking directly to you. Don't dismiss anything you read; embrace it and listen to God because He has chosen you before the foundation of the world.

Chapter 7

Your Body Is Important to God

I want to tell you why your body is important to God. A spirit can't live on earth without a body. When your body is decaying and expiring, your spirit knows it must leave because apart from the body it's illegal here. It says it must go because it can't remain here. "God created Adam from the dust of the earth" (Genesis 2:7). Therefore, the body goes back to the ground from which it came because it is part of the earth's domain. It was not made to live in the spirit realm. When God gets ready to move in the earth realm, He needs your body to get the job done. It is the protocol when you live here. Heaven only accepts your spirit, but earth needs your body for survival.

In the book of Genesis 1, God gave man dominion over the earth realm, which means God will use man here to represent Him. He put man in charge of the earth to subdue it and take care of it. That means man is in charge.

Therefore, God does not heal your body because you are so good. He heals it because He needs it to get his work done; that is why He wants you to take care of your body. He can't use a sick body full of alcohol, drugs, and diseases.

When He got ready to redeem man from sin, He put His spirit in a body to accomplish His mission. If He didn't need a body, He could have done His work from Heaven in the spirit. When you accept Christ, you give Him permission and legal access to use your body. You give God the okay to come into your earthly body on your behalf.

Satan knew earth belonged to man. Therefore, he needed a way to have legal access to dwell here. He became desperate and used the body of a snake to enter earth. No doubt, the snake was one of Eve's favorite pets. He had to use something Eve trusted. The devil is still using that same trick today. He had to find a way to catch Eve with her guards down. He only tempts you when your spirit is not charged up in prayer. Watch out for Satan when you have not spent time in prayer; it becomes your most vulnerable time for attacks.

That is how Satan got a hold of Eve. She should have had something to remind her of what God said about the forbidden tree, like the Israelites had Passover to remind them of their voyage from Egypt. Satan negotiated and tricked the snake first because it was jealous that Eve was spending too much time with the other animals and not with it.

The snake's vulnerable side allowed the devil to use its body because the snake wanted to please Eve and get her attention. The devil deceived Eve and the snake. He had been watching, planning, and plotting for Eve's fall. When the snake yielded its body to the devil, it could not warn Eve of Satan's deception. He sold his soul to the devil. Eve thought the beloved pet she trusted had her best interests in mind. Be careful whom you trust and tell your secrets to; when they get angry or jealous, the snake in them will appear.

Also, be careful what you give your attention to. If the snake had not given its attention to Satan, he would not have gained access to be here. God gave Adam and Eve a will. He doesn't work against your will. If they had been spending time in prayer, this would not have taken place. Time spent in prayer is not time wasted; it helps you to overcome temptation.

After Adam and Eve fell, God told Satan, "I will put enmity between you and the woman, and between your seed and her seed. He shall crush your head, and you shall bruise his heel" (Genesis 3:15). God is saying to Satan, you deceived a woman to get here, and I will use woman to carry my seed that will destroy you.

The seed Mary carried was God's pure blood; their blood did not mix. Mary's body was the vessel Jesus used to get here. God already had it fixed before the fall that a woman's body would carry His seed one day. Mary did not know one day she would be saved by the blood she was carrying.

God is Holy and just. God kept His word when He told Satan you used a woman to get here and it is going to be a woman that is carrying my seed that is going to crush your head and bring a savior into the earth realm to redeem man back to God.

Now do you understand why your body is important to God? He needs you to get His work done in the earth realm. When your body gets sick, ask God to heal you so He can use you to promote the gospel of Jesus Christ. He needs you to get His work done.

When God got ready to deliver his people from Egypt, He used Moses. He used Joseph to save His lineage on earth to make His entrance, and He used Jesus to redeem man from his sins. When God wanted the gospel to continue, He used Jesus' disciples. When He wanted a peace agreement for Israel, He used Donald Trump, and He is still using people today. God said, "For I know the plans I have for you, declares the Lord, plans to prosper you and not harm you, plans to give you hope and a future," (Jeremiah 29:11, NIV).

Chapter 8

Hear What God Says About Sex

Many Christians wonder what God has to say about oral sex, anal sex and masturbation. Many are struggling with this question. After reading what God says, you will be set free and delivered. Let's go to the scriptures. The Lord said, "Nevertheless, I have a few things against you: There are some among you who hold to the teachings of Balaam, who taught Balak to entice the Israelites to sin and they ate food sacrificed to idols and committed sexual immorality" (Revelation 2:14 NIV).

The teachings of Balaam were immoral sex acts and evil practices. He was a very wicked prophet in the Bible. Although he was an evil prophet, he was not a false prophet. His heart was not right in the sight of God; he betrayed Israel by leading them astray, teaching and causing them to commit abominations in the eyes of the Lord. God cursed the Israelites for their participation in immoral sex acts.

In the meantime, they were on their way to the Promised Land of Canaan. King Balak of Moab wanted to weaken them and prevent their voyage. He felt threatened while they were passing through his territory. He feared Israel's God because he had heard about what He did to other kings and nations as Israel were conquering land.

King Balak sent for, Balaam, the prophet, who lived in Mesopotamia along the Euphrates River. The king asked him to curse the Israelites in exchange for a reward. He told him he could not curse them because they were under God's protection, and the only way they could be cursed was by walking in disobedience and sin. If they obeyed God, they were in good standing with Him. The wicked prophet devised a deceitful trap to lower the children of Israel into sin.

When the men of Israel went into King Balak's camp, there were beautiful, alluring women at the camp entrance. The women lured the men into their beds and performed oral sex on them. No doubt about it, this new experience blew their minds. They also showed the men how to have sex with other men and how to pleasure themselves with masturbation. They also showed them how to have sex with animals. The Israelites took this new experience back to their camp and exposed others to this newly found sexual perversion.

It was women counseled by Balaam that caused the Israelites to sin. As a result, God removed His protection, and the enemy sent a deadly plague to them.

Through the counsel of Balaam, the children of Israel rebelled, broke faith with the Lord, and joined themselves to a sex god for pleasure. Therefore, they suffered for their disobedience.

The Prophet himself practiced immoral sex acts with his female donkey. He was exposed for his sexual immorality; it's recorded in the Book of Jubilees.

Israel joined themselves to the Sex God Baal of Peor, and the anger of the Lord was aroused against them" (Numbers

25:3 KJV). Due to their lawlessness, "twenty four thousand Israelites died" (Numbers 25:9) for their immoral practices. The plague came to a halt when a priest desecrated a midianite woman and the Israelite man that brought her into the camp. Their dead bodies were taken out of the camp.

Balaam's deceitful plan worked. He enticed the Israelites to sin; God allowed a curse to come upon Israel by removing His hedge of protection from them. And this allowed the prophet to collect his reward from the king; Balaam betrayed God for money.

Every time a believer practices sexual immorality, you defile God's laws. Unknowingly, you are joining sides with Baal Peor, a demon god. This will cause doors to open for problems in your life. As long as you practice sexual perversion, you will spend your entire life being up and down in turmoil and never coming to a stable place in your life. God's hand is off of you until you repent.

All believers should repent daily for the sins they have committed. When you keep committing the same act over again, God's grace will run out at some point. Whenever there is disobedience, punishment follows. Immoral sex acts open a demonic portal for evil spirits to attack your home with sexual perversion, confusion, poverty, lack, sickness, and disease. This spirit can transmit to your unborn offspring, and when it is conceived, it can transfer spirits of homosexuality and lesbianism to your unborn child. This act is so widely spread across the globe. It's at an all-time high as a result of having perverted sex. Don't give demonic sex spirits legal rights to enter into your life and your genealogy after you.

Unknowingly, you glorify that demonic spirit when you practice what it created. Break this generational cycle. Teach your children and family members that immoral sex acts can be dangerous, and it brings the judgment of God upon you. The judgment of God is Him removing His head of protection that covers you. God is going to hold you responsible for not teaching the truth to your children, family members, and congregations. Stay away from that which God did not create. God has mercifully covered those to whom He has given His grace. His spirit cannot dwell in an unclean temple. Keep God dwelling in your home through obedience.

Have you ever wondered why you're always having problems in your home, marriage, relationships, finances, children, and job? Sexual immorality causes God's hand to be released from you, and then the enemy has justification to curse you. It does not matter if you are filled with the Holy Ghost and water baptized. If you are participating in immorality, demonic doors have already been opened, but you can shut those doors through true repentance. If you have a problem in this area, ask the Holy Spirit to help you deny the flesh. Deliverance can begin only when you discover you have a weakness and commit to trusting God to bring you out. He did not create your mouth for sexual pleasure for the lower parts of the body, nor did He create you to arouse yourself through masturbation with or without devices. God created your mouth for tasting, eating, drinking, and speaking. He made your rear end to eliminate waste from your body, not for sexual activities.

God forbid those who say the bed is undefiled with a husband and a wife; that is correct if you don't break God's laws with sexual immorality. The act in bed has become demonic. Some Christians have corrupted what God intended to be holy in marriage. No pleasure is more significant than having God's presence. Jesus rebuked the practice of Baal of Peor, and He hated what the Father didn't create. The Lord said, "Be Ye Holy because I am Holy." If you are going to be a Christian, do so with admiration unto the Lord. Deny temptation; it only works when you give into it. God will provide you with the strength you need to do what is pleasing in His eyes. He can heal you from this addiction. If you are addicted to pornography, sincerely ask the Holy Spirit to help you overcome this addiction.

Hating the things of the flesh draws you closer to God. "If any man come after Jesus, let him deny himself, pick up your cross and follow him." That means daily denying self. The first step to deliverance is wanting it; tell yourself you will not submit to your earthly desires. Say no to the world, no to anything that hinders your walk with Christ. Immoral sex acts did not come from God, nor are they of God. Oral sex, anal sex, and masturbation are forbidden. God is faithful. He will not let you be tempted beyond what you can bear. When you are tempted, He will provide a way of escape for you.

If you have a spouse who's not willing to copulate with you because you're not willing to participate in oral sexual activities, spend time on your knees talking to the Father. He will bring your mate into alignment with what's fitting in the sight of God.

Do you understand now why your life has been like a seesaw? Today is the beginning of a new chapter in your life. Repent without condemning yourself. You have been set free from the spirit of perversion by the power of the living God that breaks every yoke in Jesus' name.

Chapter 9

How the Enemy Gains Access to You

The enemy does not have legal binding rights to you once you accept Jesus Christ as your Lord and Savior. He needs an entrance to enter any area of your life. Therefore, "the devil, as a roaring lion, walketh about, seeking whom he may devour" (1Peter 5:8). He watches for the hedges of protection to come down. The spirit of surveillance is constantly hovering over you. Sin and disobedience are the only things that can cause those hedges to come down.

The enemy is an enforcer of those who disobey God's laws. Here are some examples of what can cause your protection to be lifted: Spending time gossiping and encouraging confusion will give the enemy direct access into your family lineage to bring in chaos and disrupt family relationships. Having an adulterous affair; the penalty for it is sickness and death if you choose to stay in it without repenting and asking the Holy Spirit to bring deliverance to you. Causing someone to lose their job without just cause will give the enemy access to plague you and your family; it can keep you from having steady employment or being able to maintain and keep good-paying jobs. Opening the door to palm reading, witchcraft, watching demonic movies or demonic cartoons, listening to demonic music, reading horoscopes, lying, stealing, backbiting, sowing discord, coveting, watching pornography, and many other sins are ways the enemy gains legal rights to invade your life.

Once you receive the Holy Spirit, it will help you to overcome every temptation known to mankind. You don't have to yield to sin. Make sure you keep the door closed to sin to keep disorder out of your life.

There is a price to pay for sin. It looks and feels good for a season, but the word of God says, "The wages of sin is death." If you want to keep God's blessings flowing into your life, keep sin out and the Holy Spirit in. "The thief comes to steal, kill and destroy, I come that you might have life, and that you have it more abundantly" (John 10:10, KJV).

Chapter 10

How to Overcome Stressful Situations

The attacks of Satan start in your mind and in your present circumstances. Your mind controls every fiber of your being. If Satan controls your mind, he will control your thoughts. If you keep your eyes on your present situation, you will be trapped in a vicious cycle of defeat. Look to God who is the author and finisher of your faith, and you will become victorious. Look to Him and believe His word and promises. Use the word of God against Satan's attacks like Jesus did when He was in the Garden of Gethsemane. Satan became a defeated foe and vanished.

Satan is defeated from within when you use God's word against Him. It is a double-edged sword. "Trust in the Lord with all thy heart and lead not to your own understanding, in all your ways acknowledge Him and He will direct thy paths" (Proverbs 3:5–6 KJV).

The enemy's strategy is to attack you in vulnerable areas in your life in the situations you now face. His goal is to destroy your mind and win your soul. When you belong to God, He will make you aware of the enemy's plots, plans, and schemes before he attacks, but you must be sensitive to the Holy Spirit's warnings. Usually God will show it to you in a dream. Satan's main focus is attacking you through circumstances to create stress, which is one of his deadliest weapons. It attacks your mind, immune system, and then your body so you will become ineffective in the body of Christ. He will try to inject your mind with worry, doubt, fear, and disbelief. Beware of his vicious attacks when you worry. He wants to fill your mind with negative thoughts so you can't release your faith. When fear grips your mind, you begin to worry about your problems.

The enemy's strategy is to bombard your mind with disbelief, so that the word of God becomes ineffective in your life. How you respond to your circumstances and trials activates stress in your life. It comes when you are doubtful that God will show up and deliver you. Think back on times when you were facing troubling situations and God delivered you out of it all. No problem is too big for God. "For God has not given you the spirit of fear; but of power, and of love, and a sound mind" (2 Timothy 1:7 KJV).

Another one of the enemy's strategies is to wear you down emotionally and physically until you become weary and faint in your mind. You become defeated when you fail to fight. While you are facing turbulent situations that are beyond your human ability, stand on God's word and promises until He brings deliverance. Listen to praise and worship music; it will usher in the presence of the Lord. Don't allow discouragement to creep in; it leads to depression. Refuse to keep looking at your circumstances. Look at how big your God is, knowing that He is with you, and He will bring you out. It is only a test; prove your worthiness to believe your God. What you are facing will allow you to see God's ability and hand at work in your life. It will increase your faith, prepare you for the next battle, and cause you to work miracles like Jesus did.

You must face circumstances standing up, knowing that God will deliver you because His word says so. "God is not like man that He should lie" (Numbers 23:19 KJV). The word of God is effective when it is spoken in faith. Believe that whatever you speak will be done. Jesus has declared before leaving this earth, anything you ask the Father, He will give it to you.

Don't let Satan destroy your relationship with God and alienate you from the only one that can deliver you from your present situation. When you have a relationship with God, nothing can hurt you by any means or take you by surprise. The word of God has declared, "No weapon formed against you shall prosper" (Isaiah 54:17 KJV).

Satan's objective is to make you lose your faith in God. He wants you to question God and have Him question your loyalty to Him. Satan wants to gain control of your will so you can turn your back on God and sin against Him. God has given you a free will. The choice is yours—Heaven or hell. Remember, your victory is in your mouth. Keep your eyes on the prize and God's ability. He promised to take you step-by-step until you reach your miracle. Each step builds your faith and character in the God you serve. Know that you are in a fixed fight, and you are the winner through Christ Jesus, your Lord and Savior.

Chapter 11

How to Manage Loneliness

Loneliness is a state of being alone and feeling that you're in a situation by yourself. What has driven you to this state of mind? Is it your past, present, or future? No matter what it is, it is about to change. God is rewriting your story. Destiny is waiting on you.

Don't allow the crisis you now face to drive you out on a lonely island until you no longer recognize who you are. Be careful of suicidal thoughts. It's the number one trap Satan uses to get your soul, because he knows it's an unforgivable sin and he wins. God has a way of escape for you today. Are you in a building full of people, but you still feel alone? Loneliness is sometimes forced on you by no fault of your own but through generational curses or lingering sin. Whatever the cause may be, God has a way for you to bounce back.

Changing your attitude and disposition on life toward more positive thinking and speaking can guide you tremendously to a road of recovery. Jesus gave you a clear solution. He said, "Seek ye first the kingdom of God and his righteousness and all these other things will be added unto you" (Matthew: 6:33 KJV). When situations don't work out as planned, don't throw in the towel. Your life is not yet over. In fact, it is just beginning. He wrote the end of your story before your journey began. Maybe you didn't pass your test or get the type of job or house you wanted. Maybe you have a failed marriage, children problems, substance abuse problems, or bad parents (or perhaps you were adopted), or maybe you feel like you fail at everything you touch. It doesn't matter what caused you to be alone. It should never be an option when you're in the body of Christ. Start taking control of what enters your mind. Rebuke Satan in the name of Jesus. Don't allow him to lead you into depression on a lonely deserted island where he can play tricks with your mind and defeat you.

Stop looking for someone else to make you happy. God created you for Himself. Start looking for reasons to make God happy, and in the process, you will be happy and your days will be filled with joy. When you get it together, God will place someone in your life and use you for His Glory. Purpose is on the way; it is time for you to bounce back and enjoy the fruits of your labor while in Christ Jesus.

Here is a strategy: start quoting Bible scriptures daily. Whatever you do repetitiously becomes part of your daily routine, and it will not be a struggle for you. Find your place in God, and do whatever it is that makes you happy. Find a reason to wake up in the morning and acknowledge God first and give Him the Glory with the fruit of your lips.

These are scriptures the Lord wants you to read daily until they resonate in your spirit and your breakthrough begins:

Fear Not, for I am with you; Be not dismayed, for I am your God. I will strengthen you, yes, I will help you, I will uphold you with my right hand **Isaiah: 41:10, KJV**

Do not fear, for I have redeemed you; I have summoned you by name; you are mine, **Isaiah: 43:1, KJV**

Come unto Me, all ye who labour and are heavy laden, and I will give you rest. **Matthew:11:28, KJV**

Draw nigh to God and He will draw nigh to you **James: 4:8, KJV**

The Lord shall preserve you from all evil; He shall preserve your soul. The Lord shall preserve your coming out and going in from this time forth, and even forevermore. **Psalms 121:7-8, KJV**

But my God shall supply all your needs according to His riches and glory by Christ Jesus. **Philippians 4:19, KJV**

As I was with Moses, so I will be with thee. I will not fail thee nor forsake you. Be strong and of good courage, **Joshua:1:5-6, KJV**

Chapter 12

Your Dangerous Tongue

God doesn't take pleasure in Christians who participate in gossiping, spreading rumors, and assassinating someones character. You don't have to shoot a person with a gun to kill them, you do it with ruining their reputation and destroying their credibility with your mouth. As Christians you shouldn't do this. Use your tongue to bless someone instead of trying to destroy their character for life where others will not want to deal with them. God does not honor you nor hear your prayers when you deal with others in that manner.

This is one of the reasons you stay broken and can't get your healing. Many people have forfeited their breakthroughs by their illicit tongue, speaking those things that are not true of their brethren and those who are of God, especially the man of God. The Bible says, "Whoever keeps his mouth and tongue keeps himself out of trouble" (Proverbs 21:23 KJV). When you keep secrets told to you in confidence, it brings honor to God. It helps to determine whether God can trust you or not. Keep yourself free of spreading rumors and prejudging people; it ruins lives.

Why speak evil of people and assassinate their character by saying things of which you have no proof of the truth? The Bible says, "If anyone thinks he is religious and doesn't bridle his tongue, but deceives, this person's religion is in vain" (James 1:26 KJV). Let no corrupt talk come out of your mouth, but only to build up a person, that it may give grace to those that hear you.

Miriam, Moses' sister, got in trouble with God for her illicit tongue. She made the tragic mistake of speaking out against Moses, God's servant. The Lord heard her and struck her with leprosy. How many Christians is God judging today because they bad-mouthed His anointed vessels? God doesn't take it lightly when you speak out against someone He has anointed and appointed to do a task for Him. Your leprosy can take on many forms: sickness, death, poverty, barrenness, bad relationships, family curses, and struggles in life to achieve anything massive.

Never speak evil of someone who is experiencing setbacks, calamities, and delays. If you do, it will give Satan reasonable assurance to bring accusations against you before God for gossiping and speaking evil of someone. Things will switch; it may be their turn today, but tomorrow may be yours. If you have been guilty of this type of behavior, repent quickly before the hand of God brings judgment to your household.

All trials are not because of sin. There are trials you and your brethren face because God is growing you up, strengthening you for spiritual warfare in the body of Christ. He teaches you how to stand up against tough stuff, so you will not be driven by accusations that come your way when the enemy comes. God is about to use you. He can't use a gossiper who speaks evil of others. The Bible says, "Keep your tongue from evil and your lips from speaking deceit" (Psalms 34:13 KJV).

"A false witness will not go unpunished, and he who breathes out lies will not escape" (Proverbs 19:5 KJV). God wants all believers to understand that "You shall not spread a false report, you shall not join hands with a wicked man to be a malicious witness,"(Exodus 23:1 KJV).

Chapter 13

Have You Been Offended or Did You Offend Someone?

Being offended keeps you in a dark place because it keeps you from forgiving others. It causes you to become stagnated and hold grudges for months, maybe even years. It robs you of your peace and joy. When you are offended it's hard for you to get pass what someone has done to you. When you see them, hatred begins to build up. But, have you ever thought maybe you offended someone and they are holding something against you? Perhaps you should think about forgiving others, releasing them out of your spirit, and letting the situation go. I know what they did hurt you beyond what anyone could ever imagine. But, if you want God and others to forgive you, then you must forgive others. As long as you're holding that hurt in your heart against someone, the Holy Spirit can't do a perfect work in your life. It ties God's hand and it releases the devil's hand to cause a series of unfortunate events in your life.

Let God cleanse you and do a perfect work in you. If you are having a hard time of letting go of what someone said or did to you, read Matthew 6:14, "If you forgive other people when they sin against you, your Heavenly Father will also forgive you."

Yes, it is hard to push back and turn the other cheek sometimes. But, what if God thought like you? Jesus would have said why do I have to die on the cross for people that don't love my Father. Mankind have committed every abomination and sin under the sun.

Because God so loves you, He gave His only son for the remission of your sins. Jesus commanded that we love one another because love causes you to overlook a multitude of faults. People don't understand how a woman can keep forgiving her husband who cheats, abuses her, doesn't take care of his obligations at home and treats her poorly. It's because of the love she has for him that compels her not to hold his wrongdoings against him, but forgive him. If you practice this type of love, you would never allow offense to set in without forgiveness.

If someone offends you or you offend someone, go to that person, talk about it and get that weight off your shoulders. God wants you to be free to serve him and others. He doesn't want you carrying around the spirit of offense, that spirit is transferable, you will turn around and offend someone unknowingly. It's a viscious cycle.

It doesn't matter what it is that someone has done to offend you, go to them and get it corrected that you may live peaceably among your brethren. Holding a grudge will block your prayers in the Heavenly realm. If someone is offended by something you did them, free them up by going to them and making things right. It doesn't mean you have to be friends with them, but you're honoring what God said to do.

Having a clear conscience is very important to God, without it you can't hear the Holy spirit speak nor can it dwell richly inside of you. God wants His love to flow through you so that men can see Him through you.

Chapter 14

Listen to God's Warnings

God will always warn you before anything transpires to hinder your progress and growth in Him. If you don't understand His warnings, ask for clarity. Don't be afraid of the answer.

Jesus' disciples were afraid to ask him for clarity about the warnings He was giving them about His crucifixion. He told them on more than one occasion the son of God was going to be delivered into the hands of men to be crucified. They did not adhere to His warnings. He was revealing to them God's will for His life, so that when the time came it wouldn't take them by surprise. Never shun away from hearing truth; it is God preparing you for what awaits you up ahead.

The disciples shunned listening to Jesus as He spoke. He was going to be delivered into the hands of men, and they were going to kill Him, and then, in three days, He shall rise. They didn't understand what He was saying, and they were too afraid to ask because they didn't want to hear the truth. They wanted to hear Him say He was going to build a kingdom on earth, and they would rule and reign with Him. They had their own agenda for not listening to the warnings Jesus gave.

As a result of not knowing and understanding the will of God, they were confused and afraid. They ran for cover when Jesus was taken by the Roman soldiers. They hid behind closed doors. Don't hide in a dark room with the shades pulled down when trouble comes your way. Face the enemy head on with the assurance that you have the victory in Jesus' name.

The battles you have lost were a direct result of your not heeding God's warnings or not wanting to hear the truth of what God expects of you. The Bible says, "Seek ye first the Kingdom of God and His righteousness and all things shall be added to you" (Matthew 6:33 KJV).

Jesus was in a human body just like yours, subject to temptation and weakness. Through His obedience to God, He humbled himself. He was constantly in communion with God through prayer, fasting, and God's written word. That is how He prepared Himself and defeated Satan. He wasn't afraid to get instructions from God for His life. He wasn't concerned about God infringing upon His plans. His will became God's will. Jesus knew how to react to all situations because He was filled with the knowledge of God's agenda. And you, too, being filled with the knowledge of God's agenda, will know how to react in all situations.

In following Jesus, you must put yourself on the back burner. Find out what God is saying, and when trials come your way, you will be spiritually prepared and strong enough to handle whatever comes. You will be unstoppable and un-movable as you abide in the word of the Lord.

Allow the Holy Spirit to lead you on a fast. That is where your strength will come from. Don't go on a fast on your own. God will lead you on a fast for upcoming situations. While on a fast, pray and read the word of God. It will help you discipline yourself in the things of God. It is your weapon for any attack from the enemy. If you are not accustomed to fasting, start off with twelve hours of fasting until you are able to increase your hours and days. God will always give you the victory through your obedience. Pray in your Heavenly language if you have one. If you want one, ask God for it. The transition will be easy and rewarding.

Chapter 15

Do You Actually Know Who You Are?

Did you know you became joint heirs with Christ? It happened the moment you accepted Him into your life as your Lord and Savior. According to God's word you are "heirs of God, and joint heirs with Christ; if so be that we suffer with Him we may be also glorified together" (Romans 8:17, KJV).

Therefore, "Walk after the spirit and you will not fulfill the desires of the flesh" (Galatians 5:16, KJV). The Bible is wisdom and understanding. God wants to educate your mind and gird it with truth. He wants you to know His ways, His attributes, and how to possess supernatural powers for working miracles. As you pray daily, a transformation will begin to take place inside of you.

When you see a man or woman of God working supernatural miracles, it comes from spending time daily with the Father. You have a right to that same power because you are joint heirs with Christ. You have been chosen and adopted into God's family. An adopted child has just as much rights and privileges as a biological child; that is the law of the land in the natural and spiritual realm. You are a child of a royal priesthood. As you read the word of God, you are reading the mind of God. He will know you are His child because you will begin to look like Him in all your ways.

Provisions were prepared for you before the foundation of the world. It is like making a movie. A producer films the end of a movie before the beginning. Therefore, he already knows the outcome of the story. That is exactly what God is doing with you. All you need to do is follow the script. You are in a fixed fight, so just start thanking Him in advance. He will work out every situation in your life. Things are only rough for you because you are out of His will for your life.

Now, walk into your destiny. God loves you so much. He will defy the law of gravity to give you a miracle. He did it with Joshua when he was in a battle. He told him He was going to give him the victory. Joshua asked God to let the sun stand still, and for the moon to stop until they won the battle. The sun stopped in the middle of the sky and delayed going down for 24 hours until Israel gained the victory.

When the children of Israel were going through the wilderness, the Bible said neither their clothes nor their shoes got old. That was because God caused the atmosphere that ages things to stand still. He defied the law of gravity. The clothes and shoes grew with the children. Now, what about you? If God can cause the cosmos to stand still, He will send your expected breakthrough miracle. Take Him at His word and know that you are a child of the Highest God. Jesus said, "Anything you ask the Father in His name that He will Do" (John 14:13, KJV).

Chapter 16

Which One Are You? Natural Man,
Spiritual Man, or Carnal Man?

There are three types of Christians in the world: the natural man, the spiritual man, and the carnal man. Which one are you? When God looks at you, He doesn't see you as a certain denomination. He sees a champion in the making. He doesn't care if you are rich or poor, educated or uneducated. He sees what you will become—the finished product.

When He looks at the natural man, He sees a person who is dead in his spirit but alive in his flesh. He is disconnected from God. The natural man is spiritually dead and doesn't get any impulses from his spirit. He gets everything from his senses,—the flesh, eyes, ears and mouth; it is all about how he feels. The natural man makes you think something is from God, when it's really his flesh speaking.

Natural people wonder why you get up every Sunday morning and through the week to go to church; their understanding is unfruitful. They think it's senseless and worthless to get up in the morning and get on the prayer line when you could be sleeping; it makes no sense to them. They think it's too much church.

They think the pastor has you brainwashed. They feel that way because they are blinded from spiritual things. They are baffled by what they can't see because their spirit is dead. They respond according to how they feel at the moment. The natural man has no options. It is the Christian who is caught between two natures and the struggles going on in the mind. Until you ask God to open your eyes and change your perspective on life, you will remain a natural man.

The spiritual man has crucified his flesh and refuses to obey it. He is determined to walk in the spirit. He will not fulfill the lust and desires of his flesh. He says no to earthly desires because he is not getting any impulses from his flesh; he is not hearing them. All of his impulses are coming from the spirit realm. He's moved by what he can't see but feel. He speaks in an unknown language only God understands.

If you become a spiritual person, the world sees you as abnormal. People will think you're strange. Spiritual people help you, even though they know you don't mean them any good. They forgive people unconditionally, even when they have been used and hurt. They believe God's report over the doctor's report. They believe and start thanking God for their healing. They don't respond to what they see in the flesh; they respond to what God has said to their spirit. If He said you're going to make it, that settles it. When God says He's going to bless them, they purpose in their hearts to disagree with anything that the Lord has not spoken to their hearts. They have heard from the Lord, and they are not backing down from it. They believe God and His word rather than the situation. They believe what's coming from their spirit and not their flesh. He who has begun a good work in them shall perform it until the day of Jesus' return, so let the winds blow, the storms rage, their soul is anchored in the Lord. To be spiritual-minded is life after death.

Most people fall into the third category, the carnal man. The carnal man's mind is an enemy against God; it is deeply rooted in hatred against Him. He is not subject to the law of God, and neither can it be. They are being controlled by their fleshly desires, and they have allowed sin to control them in some area of their life. In reality, the carnal man is getting something from his flesh and something from his spirit; he is being fed from both sides and torn between two opinions. Whether you have been spending time with God will determine what opinion your life is being controlled by—something fleshly or something divine. Mostly, when life threatens you or intimidates you, and you spend time concerned with what could happen, what you could find, or what people think, you are a carnal Christian.

If you are looking at circumstances, you will never gain the victory or become the person of faith you were called to be. The battleground in life is in your mind because it is at war with the word of God. The Lord takes you through exercises. He takes you through training programs, seasons of grief. He exposes you to new levels of devils just as soon as you learn to ignore one level of devils. You keep going higher and higher in the Lord. This is a game changer.

This will change your marriage and finances. Stop paying attention to those bills and people telling you what you can't have and can't do. It is designed to mess with your mind. Make up in your heart that the promises of God are yea and amen.

Whatever it is the enemy is touching in your life, I can assure you he doesn't need it. If you wake up and discover you lost your job or home, and you said the devil did it, he did. He doesn't like your job or your home. He is after your mind, because he knows what it can do to your mind if you don't have the necessary finances to survive. Don't let your mind war against your destiny. To win the battle you must get a grip on your thinking. You must be saved in order to have options to get signals from the spirit; listen to it versus the flesh. No weapon formed against you shall prosper in any area of your life. The only hope the devil has of tripping you up is getting into your mind. But he can't have it. You are going to be renewed in the spirit of your mind, renewed in your thought process, and renewed from every distraction that comes your way. God is getting ready to do something miraculous in your life. Are you ready for it? If you want to change the world, change the way you see it. Change your perspective on the way you view life. God is trying to change you.

It doesn't matter how spiritual you are when you say you want to go higher in God. Let me tell you what's up there. The devil has some new tricks you have never encountered before to test you with. Yes, it's going to bother you until God opens your eyes and changes your perspective. The same God that delivered you when you were on the last level is the same God that will deliver you on this level. Kill the devil with your mouth and break free from the chains that have held you captive. "Walk after the spirit and you will not fulfill the lust of the flesh" (Galatians 5:16 KJV).

Chapter 17

Know Whom You Are Dealing With

Do you know whom you are dealing with? Instinct alone is not enough for spiritual warfare. Let me give you a brief snapshot of the enemy you are encountering. He is an archangel that is a general over fallen angels. We wrestle in life with our flesh, leaders in authority, powers and principalities in this present world. They rule over regions and territories. There are archangels, and then there are lower-level angels. Therefore, what you have is a devil in charge with power. He had God-given authority in Heaven; his powers were ordained by God. He was in a leadership position.

When God gives you a position with authority, and you abuse that power, He will pull you down from your position of leadership. The book of Isaiah mentions an angel that had a leadership position in charge of praise and worship that fell down suddenly to a low state. How is it something that was so high ended up so low, weakening the nation? Here is the answer to that question. It is broken down into five components on how Lucifer fell.

First, he said, "I will ascend into the Heavens." He got lifted up in pride.

Second, he said, "I will go beyond what my God has allotted." He wanted more authority than God gave him.

Third, he fell into covetousness. He wanted to replace God. If you find yourself wanting something that belongs to someone else, watch out! That's not of God; that's your ungodly nature. If the spirit of covetousness has gripped you, shake it off. If you don't, you're setting yourself up for a fall.

When someone goes to you before they go to God, that is a dangerous place to be. Make sure you redirect their thought pattern to check in with God first, and if God leads them back to you, then pray for them.

Fourth, he said, "I will sit upon the mount of the congregation on the side of the north." That spot is designated for God. When God kicked Satan out of Heaven, He put him out on the north side, where he tried to set up his kingdom. Satan wanted to be the supreme ruler in Heaven and on earth.

Fifth, he said, "I will ascend above the heights of the clouds and I will be like the Highest God." He wanted God's position, power, and authority in Heaven. In life you are always confronted with someone who wants to take your place in some sort of capacity.

It was Satan's "I will" that led to his expulsion from Heaven. Everyone is confronted with the I will test, even Christ. He prayed, "Father not my will, but thy will be done." It will always be God's will or your will, and your loyalty to Him will be put to the test. He will always give you the choice to choose right or wrong.

The quickest way to move into the things of God is to humble yourself, and God will exalt you. Desire the things of God, and you will move in such a dimension until things will become subject to you. The fastest way to die in God is to become arrogant and high-minded. The more you humble yourself, the more God will raise you up. Many of your prophesies and blessings have been held up and delayed, and you have blamed other people. It is your attitude that is destroying you, and until you fix it, you will not go anywhere in God. You don't have that type of time to waste. Search your heart for the will to go up, especially when it comes to kingdom going-up.

Position seekers will never be successful in God. When you pursue God with ambitious motives, you frustrate the grace of God. It insults Him to know you are in His face for ulterior motives. God wants you to be here for Him. Don't let the enemy distract you into any other pursuits than the kingdom of God. He will take you up, and He can take you down. Anything you want more than God becomes an idol in your life.

The spirit of Saul has entered the church. When Saul became king of Israel, he didn't try to get the Ark of the Covenant back that had been gone for twenty years. He was more concerned with a position from God. He wasn't concerned about having the presence of God.

God sent Samuel to judge Saul, and the kingdoms were taken from his hands. Saul said, "I gave sacrifices, and God said obedience is better than sacrifice." God told him, "I have found me a man that is after my heart."

David went after God's heart, and it was noted he became the apple of God's eye. He wanted God's presence. He never wanted a position, and God made him king over all of Israel. God will reject any man who wants a position more than His presence, because it reminds Him of Lucifer. When God sees that, He will yank the position and give it to someone who is worthy but less qualified. He will raise them up because they are after His heart and not a position. Instead of Satan being satisfied with being in charge of praise and worship, he wanted to be worshiped.

Jesus said, "The enemies of this world came against me to try me but have found nothing in me." There is nothing the enemy can do to you when you purge your heart of illicit desires. The enemy won't have anything to work with because all you want to do is base yourself in the presence of the Lord.

If you conceal any of the I will in your heart, the devil will keep you up all night praying, trying to manipulate God into giving you a position without His presence. Manipulation destroys trust. It's not of God. There are many pastors and priests holding positions without God.

Get into a place in Him where you can be effective and bring about a change wherever you go. When two believers get together, powerful things happen. God will give you enough power to bring change to cities and laws in legislation. Demon powers will become subject to you and dismantled.

Turn loose distractions, turn over your plate, shut the TV and cell phone off, and spend time with God and His word. It's food for your spirit. Don't assume you have mastered God's word. Read it like you're looking for treasure. Every time you read, you will get a fresh revelation. When you know God's word for yourself, no one can pluck the truth out of you. Be vigilant in your studies. When trouble arises, the word in you will minister to your spirit.

Chapter 18

The Real Purpose of the Church

The purpose of the church is established by God as a Holy Convocation where souls are saved and Christians gather to learn the scriptures, worship, pay tithes, bring sacrificial gifts to the altar, and assist the poor. It is a house of prayer. Every church should have a boiler room where intercessory prayer goes on twenty-four hours a day. People's needs should be met by the supernatural power of God every time the doors are opened. There should be ongoing ministry to meet the needs within the church. Salvation and healing should be taking place. The broken-hearted, wounded souls should be ministered to and healed by the power of God. The church is a place of refuge for the homeless. There should be miracles taking place daily as a normal course of action.

God never intended for His people to go to church and get their spirits wounded from the pulpit. Many pastors have caused babies in Christ to backslide by slandering them from God's pulpit. They need healing for their souls when the world gets finished beating up on them. It's okay to correct what you see wrong in the church. But do it out of love and not with an arrogant spirit. Don't purpose in your heart to wound a Christian; you have to give an account to God for misrepresenting Him.

Today, many of the large churches have turned into money-making corporations that are more concerned about financial gain than fulfilling the purpose God intended for the church. Jesus had a definite opinion on what the work of the church should look like and the purpose it serves.

On two occasions He cleansed the temple of money changers and those who were buying and selling. The first occasion was at the beginning of His ministry. He went to Jerusalem during Passover and went into the temple. He found it polluted with money changers and people who were selling sheep, oxen, and doves for sacrificial offerings. When He saw this, He was filled with righteous indignation. He overturned the tables of money changers. He made a whip from a cord, and ran everyone out of the temple. Jesus was angry at what He saw. He said to the people in the temple, "How dare you turn my Father's house into a market" (John 2:16 NIV). They were making a profit on the things that belonged to God through their buying and selling of animals for sacrifices. Corrupt men had turned the temple courts into a marketplace where they were making merchandise of things that were to be dedicated to God. The greedy money changers were there charging the poor exorbitant fees to exchange money into silver required for the temple treasury. All of this was going on in the house of God, much like today when activities are going on in churches to raise money that doesn't befit meeting the needs of the poor, widows, and the house of God.

Jesus is still overturning tables by shutting down churches and allowing the judgment of God to come upon them. The house of God is being used for many things: meeting places for men to meet women, places for pastors to have sex with members of their congregations, places where people engage in homosexuality, lesbianism, fornication, business deals, manipulation, and stealing church offerings. Jesus sees all of this going on in the house of God today.

On the second occasion, Jesus cleansed the temple the final week before He went to the cross. Every step and action He took that week was with divine purpose. The temple had once again become polluted, and it was meant with opposition. Jesus went to reestablish the church. He wanted the people to know the true purpose and meaning for the temple. Once He drove the buyers, sellers, and money changers out, He began to teach the people: "There was an awesome release of the miracles by the power of God. The blind and lame went to Jesus in the temple, and He healed them there." The message Jesus was conveying is that this is what should be going on in My Father's house. Many miracles took place once the temple was cleansed. God is saying that many signs and wonders will take place once pastors cleanse God's house of corruption and pollution.

Churches spend too much time raising money for selfish reasons. Pastors have become too greedy. They find themselves trying to see who can buy the finest car or the biggest house. Some churches have become recreation centers or shows for the latest fashions and attempts to out-dress the pastor and the first lady. A lot of Christians today have "a form of Godliness but denying the power thereof" (2 Timothy 3:5 KJV). Churches have become social centers with activities. That may be good in its time and season, but it isn't what God had in mind for His church.

Prophets are giving revivals and charging people exorbitant prices to give them prophecies that largely never happen. This is not pleasing to the Lord. Ministries are in competition over who can build the largest building or draw the biggest crowd. When all of these things take place, God is moved with indignation and begins to overturn things in the body of Christ. He will purge the church that has become polluted with carnal desires, selfishness, covetousness, fraud, and other ungodly attributes.

What Jesus is seeing now doesn't coincide with the purpose of the church. God is calling for corrective action for those who are going to represent Him in the body of Christ. Those ministries that refuse to submit to doing things God's way in the area of finances and helping God's people will not take part in His spiritual blessings.

Chapter 19

The Reasons Jesus Came to the Earth Realm

Jesus came down in the form of human flesh to declare the promises of a new covenant He came to establish. As a messenger, He proclaimed the conditions and the terms. He gave specific promises to those who were obedient to God's word. He explained how you would become one with Him and partake of all His blessings. In the new covenant, Jesus made it possible for you to go directly to the Father, and ask whatever you need, in His name, and you will receive it. God blessed and prospered Israel greatly under the old covenant which was based upon sacrificing the blood of bulls and goats. Today, according to the new covenant, God will bless you even more which is sealed and made effective through the blood of Jesus. As long as you are following the will of God for your life, the sky is the limit in what you can ask for. Because the Holy spirit will not allow you to ask for something totally out of the will of God for your life.

For the new covenant to be established, it was necessary for Christ to offer up Himself as the perfect and only sacrifice sufficient to redeem man from sin and destroy the works of the devil. Through Jesus' death, broken body, and shedding of His blood, the new covenant was put into effect. As a believer, whatever you ask the Father in Jesus' name, it shall be granted according to (John 16:23-24 KJV). Every promise Jesus made up until now has been been kept. When you understand the power and authority that's behind that name, then you can see all of heaven backing you up when you ask for what it is you need in Jesus' name. If you need healing for your body, finances, situations to turn around, peace from losing a loved one, no matter what it is Jesus said ask the Father and it will be given to you. However, you must be walking in obedience to God and His word to proclaim the blessing of asking. Supernatural miracles are performed using Jesus' name. It's just like having a rich Father who owns a chain of stores, and he tells the manager of one of the stores to give you whatever you ask for using his name. Likewise with our Heavenly Father.

Jesus declared, "If a person loves me, he will keep my word, and My Father will love him, and We will come to him and make our home with him" (indwelling of the Holy Spirit).

There is only one way to enter a blood relationship with God, and that is through Jesus. It is through Him you receive the promise of eternal inheritance. God placed His spirit within you to dwell in Him. He made you His very own sons and daughters. After Adam lost the presence of God, He promised to redeem you and give His Holy Spirit to you, that you may have fellowship with Him. When you have the Holy Spirit dwelling richly in you, sin has no power over you. The only power it has is your will through temptation. Through His spirit you have the power not to yield to sin. Before the Holy Spirit, Satan had the power to attack your mind. Now, you have the Holy One dwelling in you; all of Satan's powers are broken. With God's spirit in you now, you are one with Him.

He placed His spirit within you to lead and guide you into all truth, reveal His will for your life, and reveal all things He has prepared for you. Now that you know the Holy Spirit lives inside of you, you have the ability and power to walk in obedience to God. One of the conditions you must meet to claim His promises is that you must love other members of the body of Christ. Your love shouldn't fluctuate up and down with your emotions. Jesus' love is supposed to manifest through you and remain the same. It is Jesus' love that is going to draw men unto you.

He placed His spirit in you, giving you supernatural gifts of the spirit to minister healing and deliverance to the world. Through His spirit, He gave you Dunamis power over the enemy, power over sin, and power to conform you into the exact image of Him. Because Jesus went to the Father, we now have power and authority in His name. He said, "I solemnly tell you, If anyone steadfastly believes in me, he will himself be able to do the things that I do; and he will do even greater things, because I go to the Father, And whatsoever you ask in my name, that I will do, that the Father may be glorified in His Son: And If you love me keep my commandments" (John 14:12–15 KJV).

Jesus is saying that He gave you His name, which represents all that He is, forever yours. He said, "Ye have not chosen me, but I have chosen you, and ordained you, that ye should go forth and bring forth fruit" (John 15:16 KJV).

Chapter 20

God Requires You to Pay Tithes

Tithing is part of a divine plan ordained by God. It is essential for you to understand why tithing is so important to God and why it's important for you to tithe. God set tithing into order through Abram paying tithes to the priest Melchizedek, the King of Salem (descendant of Noah), four hundred years before the law of Moses was ever established. It set the precedent for tithing. God reemphasized paying tithes through the law of Moses because the people of God had gotten away from it, and God wanted to show them how to be blessed and keep a continuous flow of His blessings in their lives.

Tithing is a Holy act unto the Lord. It is an act of worshiping Him. His major purpose for requiring tithes is so His people could learn to recognize Him as their main source and acknowledge their dependence upon Him. When you give your money, it is God's method of pouring His blessings upon you. As you offer your tithes freely to Him, you are honoring Him as your source. When you sacrifice and give money that you need to God, it pleases Him just as Abram pleased Him when he was willing to offer up Isaac to Him. That showed God the measure of love Abram had for Him because Abram put what God wanted first. Through Abram's diligence, God blessed him beyond measure—more than he could imagine. His seed is still reaping the benefits from the sacrifices he made to God.

When you give your offerings to God with a pure heart in faith, He will manifest His power on your behalf. You can leave the altar with absolute assurance that God's blessings will be released in your life, and He will supernaturally meet your needs. Tithing is for your benefit. Is it a command from God? Yes, it is. The choice is yours. When you give to the poor, you're giving to God. His blessings will flow into your life. Giving to God works for the just and the unjust.

God no longer wants to bless His people through animal sacrifices. It became too polluted. The major methods He uses today are your money and your time. And the money must be allocated to good use.

The prophet Malachi was used to reemphasize the order of tithing. When the children of Israel were tired of living under a closed Heaven, they cried out to the Lord, and He sent Malachi to tell them, "Bring ye all the tithes into the store house that it may be food in my house and prove me to see if I will open up the windows of Heaven and pour you out blessings you won't have room to receive" (Malachi 3:10 KJV).

As the creator of the universe, God does not need your money. But He does require your obedience to be blessed. All the wealth in the world belongs to Him. However, nothing will leave Heaven until something leaves earth first. Putting God first is how you honor Him.

Your tithes are to help support the ministers of the Gospel of Jesus Christ. The apostles, prophets, pastors, evangelists and teachers are your modern-day Levites that God has raised up to give themselves solely to the work of God. They are placed within the church and given the responsibility of building up and bringing the body of Christ to full maturity. God doesn't demand your money like a dictator. A tenth of your money and time proves your loyalty to God as you give what is required of you. When you obey God, you don't have to face financial crisis alone. His word said to prove to him. God is at His best when you face circumstances you can't handle.

Solomon understood the key to financial blessings when he said, "Honor the Lord with thy substance, and with the fruits of all thy increase: so, shall thy barns be filled with plenty" (Proverbs 3:9–10, KJV). He was the richest and wisest man who ever lived—surely you want to take his advice!

In churches today, pastors manipulate people into giving; that is considered a polluted offering. It will not be accepted by God, nor will you be blessed. God is overturning this type of altar. Instead of Him pouring out His blessings, a curse will be poured out. He will not curse you, but he will take His hand off of you, and the devil will bring a curse to you because he has reasonable cause for his actions. The enemy can plague your finances through disobedience if you refuse to pay your tithes. It is in the Old Testament and the New Testament. God uses tithing to bless His people and put a hedge of protection around their finances.

God wants His people to give with willing hearts. He takes pleasure in His people bringing sacrificial offerings with pure hearts and right intentions. Before bringing your money to the altar, ask God to forgive you for all your sins; this is a requirement before you put your money on the altar. This paves the way for your tithes to be accepted by God. It will cause the Angels to come down with your miracles, and your prayer requests will be granted.

Chapter 21

Reasons Why God Requires You to Take Communion

Communion is called the Lord's supper. It is a covenant meal that activates promises with God. Jesus told His followers to do this in remembrance of Him; it was a command. The early church received incredible miracles after taking communion. This activates every promise made by God. This is a mystery meal with Him. It is the only physical meal you take with Him. It connects Heaven with earth. It is an entrance into God's covenant blessing plan. His love unites you to Him. It is an invitation into His Heavenly realm.

In this meal, bread represents Jesus' body, and the wine represents His blood. If you no longer see bread but rather see it as His body, it heals you of every illness in your body. If you see the wine as His blood, you begin to enter a new world with Christ. You have a new life in Him. All sins are forgiven. When you drink, you partake of His suffering for you. In the spirit you drink His blood and eat to become part of Him.

When Jesus took communion with His disciples in the upper room before His death, He wasn't just establishing a religious ceremony for the church to follow. He was offering His life. The meal was a symbol of Himself. The wine they drank together represented His blood that He would shed so they could be bound together with Him and each other. This union is stronger than a mother's natural birth union to a child.

Jesus was trying to explain to His disciples the rationale behind communion—how things come alive when you partake in this ceremony. When you don't understand communion, you are in danger of polluting this meal. He wanted you to focus and do this in remembrance of Him, not just see it as a meal. Therefore, remember the price He paid in pouring out His blood and the death of His body for your sake. Every time you take communion, your body is supposed to be healed of all manner of diseases. There is a stipulation to this; you must be walking in obedience to His will.

Most Christians are sick today because they have not discovered the relevance of taking communion, and they take it when they are unworthy. Men are missing out because they don't understand this mystery. They see it as something symbolic or traditional. There is forgiveness, healing, restoration, life, and so much more at the Lord's supper. There is spiritual life in the wine when you drink it.

When you take your communion, make a covenant with God and keep it; He will surely keep His part of the contract. God made a covenant with Abram when he was seventy-five years old. Twenty-four years had passed, and the contract was not sealed. When dinner was served, God declared that Isaac would be born the next year. He was born nine months later. Every covenant God made in the Bible was sealed at dinner after a meal. God will make and keep covenants with you after taking the Lord's supper; this is one of the benefits of taking communion. Every time you take it, you renew your covenant that was made with God. He will not only answer your prayers, but also He will add abundant prosperity to your life.

As you take your communion, remember that Jesus said, "For as often as you eat this bread and drink of this cup, you proclaim the Lord's death until He comes" (1 Corinthians 11:26, NIV). Jesus was saying you can take the Lord's supper as often as needed, especially when you want to make a covenant with Him. It is a sure way to get your prayers answered.

Chapter 22

Reasons Your Prayers Go Unanswered

God hears your prayers the moment you pray. But there is an unseen barrier that's tying God's hand where he can't violate His laws and bless you. It is called evil portals and altars. Many of God's people wonder why their prayers are not answered. It's an unseen force that has been given permission to carry out its mission on seeing your demise. Destroy those evil assignments and generational curses that come through open portals.

Jesus shed seven drops of blood for our prayers to be answered. Unanswered prayers start when you disobey God. It first started when Adam and Eve fell from grace in (Genesis 3). God said, cursed is the ground for thy sake; in sorrow shalt thou eat of it all the days of thy life (Genesis 3:17);18 Thorns also and thistles shall it bring forth to thee; and thou shalt eat the herb of the field (Genesis 3:18).19 In the sweat of thy face shalt thou eat bread, till thou return unto the ground; for out of it wast thou taken: for dust thou art, and unto dust shalt thou return (Genesis 3:19). Which means you will struggle to survive, work two and three jobs just to pay your bills, work without enjoying the fruit of your labor, spending more time at work than with your spouse and children.

To reverse the curse pronounced on man, Jesus sweated drops of blood from His face like tears, which represented man would not have to struggle to survive all the days of his life, living only to exist.

Second: Matt 26:63-67 Jesus was Struck on His Face with fits and rods, which destroys the spirit of slander off your life.

Third: Isaiah 50:5-6 The hair on His Beard was pulled out. This is to destroy the spirit of shame.

Fourth: Matthew 27:26 Strips of blood on his back, represented by His strips you can get your healing through Him using His name.

Fifth, Matthew: 27:29 Crowns of thorns pressed into His scalp, this is to take away poverty.

Sixth, Matthew 27:35 Nails in His hands and feet, this is to restore man spiritually back to God.

Seventh, John:19:34, Pierced in His Side for those who are hurt, wounded and broken hearted and in mourning

Ask the Father in Jesus' name to issue a restraining order against Satan and his cohorts in Jesus' name, and keep you protected and covered with His blood. Ask that all accusations against you be dropped. Then you will begin to live a long, happy, and prosperous life.

Chapter 23

Understanding the Purpose of Prayer, Praise & Worship

When you understand the purpose of prayer, you begin to understand the mind of God. He wants you to communicate and have fellowship with Him. When you read the word of God, it draws you into His spiritual world, you begin to take on His qualities; you think, act, and speak the way that is pleasing unto Him.

Spending time with God feels like two people in love being intimate with each other. What a great feeling to be in love with your God, knowing He will take care of you. God wants you to cast everything you are facing in life upon Him, because He care's for you. "Love the Lord your God with all your heart and with all your soul and with all your mind" (Matthew 22:37, KJV). He wants to talk to you by holding a conversation with you. Before you know it, you will start glowing. The presence of the Lord will be all around you.

Moses started glowing when he spent time embracing God. Now, what about you? As you spend time with Him, the things of this world will no longer hold your interest; they will be things of the past, and you will be a new creature in Christ Jesus.

God is saying these things to you today: I wish you would talk to Me. I wait for you every day to commune with Me. I want you to know Me and My ways. I want the mind of Me to be in you. I gave you My Holy Spirit for you to become one with Me. Man could not communicate with Me after Adam's spiritual death until I sent my son, Jesus, which paved the way for this door to be opened. Now, walk through it!

The more you spend time in God's presence, the more you will want to stay there. In Him there is love, joy, peace, happiness, and fulfillment. As you begin to pour into Him, sickness has to flee your body because you're in His presence. Your flesh is of this world, but when you are in His midst, it is subject to your command and controlled by the Holy Spirit that dwells richly inside of you because you spend time with the Father. Time with Him is not time wasted.

Start interceding for others in your prayer language, and the Lord will cause you to go higher in Him. When you travail before the Lord, He will bring you to a place high and lifted up in Him. He will bring you into a realm that will confuse the enemy, and he will not be able to track or trace you in the realm of the spirit. God will give you staying power, holding power, and prevailing power. He will give you enormous working power. He will give you power to heal the sick and raise the dead. When you travail before the Lord, He will give you access to what other church goers don't have. He will give you authority over territories and regions where the enemy has set up camp. When you travail and praise God, it pushes the enemy back across the line he illegally crossed. It gives you legal authority to command the enemy to release everything that belongs to you and others. You become the catalyst on the hill that God has ordained for such a time as this. You're not God's less; you're God's best. Satan will have to go into his trophy room, where he has things that have been stolen from the people of God. I want you to know Satan has a room full of things on display that he has stolen from the people of God. He brags about how easy it was to take them. He has your joy, peace, loved ones, marriage, children, house, car, business, money, job, bank account, and so much more. But when you travail before the Lord, it breaks that thing in the spirit realm. Satan has to release what he's stolen, and then he has to pay double dividends. God Himself is going to command Satan to cough it up, spit it out, release it, and let it go. That's the benefit of travailing before the Lord.

When God shows you someone's face in your spirit, immediately start praying for that person. Satan has stolen something from that person who needs a breakthrough or a miracle. And you have been given the assignment to pray fervently for them until you feel a release in your spirit.

When you enter into the area of praise & worship it changes the dynamic of your sphere in the spirit realm. Things and situations come alive and become subject to you for the gospel's sake. The presence of God meets you there because He dwells there. It is the secret place of the most high God. You feel His presence as a breath of fresh air. Thoughts of unasked prayers are granted. God becomes a light to guide your feet. He becomes your covering, shield and protector in a time of need. He tramples on your enemy for His name's sake. He put fire walls and smoke screens to hide you from your enemies. There is no situation under the sun that will overtake you. As you awake in the morning and throughout the day, allow praise and worship to be in your heart towards God. Keep God near you all the day long. When it's time to pray it won't take you all day to feel His presence.

Chapter 24

Spiritual Garments Required by God for Every Believer

Every believer is mandated to put on spiritual warfare garments to be armed, alert, and ready for action. It is essential to be prepared so you will never experience defeat in any circumstance or situation you face in life. You will be victorious and win every battle as you face it head on. You will be unbeatable, unmovable, and unstoppable when you put on the required spiritual armor of God. These were the garments Jesus and His disciples put on when they started their earthly ministry.

God revealed to the Apostle Paul the spiritual garments to put on while he was chained to a Roman solider in prison. He wrote to the church of Ephesus and gave them specific instructions on how to arm themselves in this life. He declared once you become a Christian you are drafted into God's army as a soldier. He wanted all believers to know how easy and simple it is to defeat the enemy once you are properly girded with truth and spiritual weapons of mass destruction.

The first spiritual garment of preparation is repentance. God can't dwell in a sinful body. You must ask Him to forgive you of all sin and iniquity that so easily beset you. Through faith in Christ's death and resurrection, you are acquitted of all charges against you and any wrongdoings on your part. You have peace knowing that the blood of Jesus has cleared you. Now, it's time to move forward.

The second spiritual garment is the Helmet of Salvation. Believe that "There is no other name under heaven given to mankind whereby you must be saved" (Acts 4:12 NIV). Accept the name of Jesus. Salvation involves more than forgiveness of your sins. It includes justification, sanctification, and deliverance from the power of sin. It includes all the blessings God has given men through the Holy Spirit.

Ask the Father in Jesus' name to allow the Holy Spirit to dwell richly in you and become one with Christ. Now, the spirit that's in Jesus lives in you. Now, you can walk upright and blameless before God. The Holy Spirit will only convict you when you are walking contrary and disobedient to God's will. It comes to help you stay on the right course. It won't allow you to walk contrary to God's plan for your life.

The third spiritual garment is the Breastplate of Righteousness. In Christ, you are justified and declared righteous because you have had your sins cleansed by Jesus. Your past sins and all your present and future sins that you have repented are covered in God's grace. The moment you received Christ, you were clothed in righteousness, not because of your goodness but because you are restored to a position of holiness and righteousness God intended for you to have. You begin to live as a born-again believer. Walk in obedience to God and the Father through Jesus Christ as the Holy Spirit leads and guides you in your everyday walk. Put away lying, cheating, manipulation, stealing, backbiting, evil thoughts, evil heart, selfishness, mean spirit, bad attitude, coveting, arrogant spirit, and a prideful look. Walk in love and peace with all men. Love one another as Christ loves the church. Without righteous living, you don't have on your spiritual garments, and you leave yourself open for Satan's attack. He is always looking for the hedges of protection to come down so he can attack you with accusations against you before God.

The fourth spiritual garment is the Girdle Belt of Truth. To clothe your mind in truth, you must abide in the word of God. It must remain in you. His word is truth and a lamp unto your feet. The gospel of truth sets men free. You must be truthful and honest in everything you do and with everyone. Don't become a hypocrite. When you hear God's word being preached, measure it by the word in you for truth. Search the scriptures and believe not every man, regardless of who it is. Many are led astray by not knowing God's word. God is looking for people who will worship Him in spirit and in truth, always. Make sure you are sincere in your relationship with God. To stand firm against Satan's attacks, you must know the truth (God's word) and come into full understanding and accurate knowledge of the son of God. The Holy Spirit that abides in you proceeded from God and will guide you into all truth. He is transforming you right now into Christ's image. As you are clothed in Him, you believe by faith you have the written and living word abiding in you. You are prepared and ready at all times to face and proclaim the Gospel of Jesus Christ to a lost and dying world.

The fifth spiritual garment is the Shield of Faith. When truth (God's word) is revealed to you, it activates your faith. This faith will release God's power into action. Whatever you ask the Father in Jesus' name will be done. As a believer and in right standing with God, you have a legal right to use Jesus' name. All the power and authority in Heaven is backing you up in His name. You are invoking the power to bring about what you desire according to the will of God. When you call Jesus' name, you put into operation the authority and power that is in that name to bring healing and any kind of deliverance to God's people, just by asking. Jesus shows up in His name. No doubt. He said, "Anything you ASK the Father in my name, shall be done of my Father" (John 16:23, KJV).

The sixth spiritual garment is the Boot or Sandal. It is a very vital part of a soldier. It helps him to stand firm during battle while fighting. A soldier plants his feet firmly on the ground to keep from slipping. In the spiritual realm, your boot represents the gospel of peace. Your feet carry the whole body. Without it, you're unable to fight in battle. The devil wants you to worry and doubt God's word so you will not be able to reach out to God by faith and grab hold of the miracles you need. The gospel of peace covers your heart and mind. Jesus purchased your peace with His blood. It strengthens you and prepares you for spiritual warfare. In having God's peace, you are unconquerable, bold, fearless, and ready to face any obstacles that await you. Peace is God's assurance when losing a loved one; winning the battle over worry, anxiousness, fear, loneliness, sickness, and lack of finances; losing a job, home, car, or business; experiencing marital problems, divorce, or lowliness; and facing every danger when confronting death. When your mind is attacked, you will be strong and untouchable. You must always keep on the gospel of peace to cover your mind and heart. His peace goes beyond your peace. He gives you supernatural peace when facing an adversary. When situations arise, you are not moved by your emotions because you know "God will keep you in perfect peace because your mind is stayed on Him" (Isaiah 26:3 KJV). Without peace, you will be weakened and not win the battles. Remember, Jesus purchased our peace with His blood. It will strengthen and sustain you when anything comes into your mind to attack it. You have the power to dismiss it immediately in Jesus' name. That's the advantage you have over Satan. He can't work against your will because it is forbidden by God.

The seventh piece of garment is the Sword, the Word of God. When the Apostle Paul talked about the Roman soldier's sword, he was talking about the Rhema word. Spoken directly to you from God, it becomes a powerful weapon in the believer's mouth. With it comes the faith you need. As you speak it out, it will destroy the enemy's strongholds. The sword, the Rhema word, is a powerful weapon God provided that makes you not only invulnerable to Satan's attacks but also able to conquer an enemy that has already been defeated. Jesus defeated him by speaking the word of God against his attacks. That's why it is so important to know the scriptures to speak against Satan during combat. The word becomes a mighty, double-edged sword.

As an end-time spiritual warrior, you must pick up your sword to defeat Satan and cleanse yourself of all unrighteousness through the word of God.

The Holy Spirit speaks through the word.It cuts through and penetrates deep into the heart and removes those sinful thoughts, lust of the flesh, and hidden sins from your heart. You can't see the sins in your life of disbelief, bitterness, hatred, jealousy, and pride that are hidden in your heart. But it's easy for you to see sin in someone else's life. Using the Rhema word, the Holy Spirit is working in you today to cleanse and purge you of all sin and disbelief. The Holy Spirit, through His word, cuts through and penetrates deep into the heart and exposes the sin that's there.

During Jesus' life on earth, He confronted Satan and defeated him. He had been commissioned, sent forth, and anointed by God to destroy the works of the devil. You, too, have been commissioned, sent forth, and anointed by God to destroy the works of the devil. Everywhere Jesus encountered the works of the enemy, He took authority over him by speaking the word. The words that came from His mouth were powerful, lethal weapons hitting the mark and driving Satan out. Evil spirits are powerless in His presence. Jesus spoke the word and destroyed Satan's strongholds. You can speak the word and destroy his stronghold in your life and in the lives of others.

The Apostle Paul told the Ephesians to be clothed in the whole armor of God. That means having on all the spiritual garments you need to enter a spiritual union with Christ, in which you are one with Him. Christ is in you, and you are in Him. Stand before the enemy perfected, fully equipped in the fullness of Christ. As you are clothed in Him, you can withstand every fiery dart of the enemy. You can endure suffering, persecutions, temptations, trials, and testing, and you can be 100% victorious. To enter this union, Christ's word must be continually in you. It should not depart out of your heart or mind. The word should come alive in you as much as the air you breathe.

Your union with Christ does not develop by being in church every time the doors open. He must be your first love. Your greatest desire must be to live every moment of your life in fellowship with Him. Every moment in which you walk in complete obedience, you draw strength from Him. Every moment in which he manifests Himself through you, it will flow to your family, friends, coworkers, and all those with whom you come into contact with.

There is no reason for you to be without your armor. You will know that you are fully equipped when you are not so easily led into temptation. Never be caught without your garments. The moment you fail to abide in God and His word, you will become vulnerable to Satan's attacks.

Chapter 25

How to Honor God

Honor God with the fruit of your lips. Honor him with praise, worship, righteous living, obedience to Him and His word, being kind to one another, allowing love to flow through you, forgiving one another, helping those that are in need, putting others before yourself, supporting ministries, being grateful, paying your tithes, giving thanks and love offerings, forgiving yourself, trusting Him with your whole heart always, and studying your reference bible. Pray for yourself and others, deny the flesh, be thankful always and follow after the spirit of God. When you do all those things, then you are truly honing and serving the God that made the earth His footstool, who is an incredible God.

Come before God with a pure heart and pure motives. Make sure you ask Him to forgive you for all sin and iniquity. Enter into His courts with praise and thanksgiving. Truly God inhabit the praises of His people. When you have done all theses things you are honoring the God that said He will provide and protect us from the snares of our enemies.

Chapter 26

Take it Back, Now!

Take back everything the devil has stolen from you. God has given you jurisdictional authority over realms, regions, your communities, cities, states and countries. When there is a lot of crime going on in a neighborhood, that means there is demonic activity in the atmosphere, hovering over that neighborhood, influencing people to commit crimes. God has given you the power and authority to decree and declare victory over evil in your neighborhood, to shut it down, and run the devil out of business. A christian shouldn't have to move and leave their home because of a drug infested area. Take authority over that demon and clean up your neighborhood. Take authority over the spirit that is hovering on your job, in your family, your business, and your marriage.

In (Daniel 6:10 & 9:3 KIV) there was an invisible war going on in the Heaven, not seen by the naked eye. Daniel prayed three times a day. But a particular prayer request was delayed for twenty-one days. Just like a demon was holding up Daniel's prayer request. Likewise, what have you prayed for that seems to be held up?

The answer to Daniel's prayer was held up because the Prince of the Kingdom of Persia ruled and had dominion over Persia and did not want to relinquish its demonic powers. The Prince of Persia was a demonic spirit that set up camp in the atmosphere over the entire region of Persia. The nation was under its demonic influence. Daniel prayed that God would spare the desolation of Jerusalem. Daniel thought the time had come for Jerusalem to go into seize and captivity for seventy years under the Persian's rule.

The demonic spirit did not want it to be known to Daniel that the interpretation of the prophecy was about the Messiah that was coming. Therefore, when God sent the understanding of the prophecy with Gabriel to Daniel, it was intercepted by demonic forces. God sent, Michael, the Arch Angel, to assist Gabriel with the heavenly war that was in motion. There are wars constantly going on in the atmosphere on your behalf that your naked eye can't see.

Take authority and prepare yourself through prayer for warfare. Once you are spiritually armed, you are ready for spiritual battles with reinforcement from angelic beings. The first line of defense in any area of your life that the devil is touching is prayer. The artillery for you to use through tough situations is fasting. The greater the battle, the more you will need the two working together.

Chapter 27

Now, Do You Believe You Were Sent and Called by God?

Yes, God has called you. Your time is now. He named and called you for a time such as this like He did Moses. When God sent Moses to deliver His people from the bondage of the Egyptians, he asked God, "Who shall I say sent me?" He replied, "Tell them I am that I am sent you" (Exodus 14 KJV).

How many people can say, "God sent me"? Not many. All ministers are not sent from God. Many of them sent themselves because they were motivated by money. Preaching has become a big money-making business, especially if you are prophesying.

God sent you. Will you obey the calling? The choice is yours to obey or not. He placed His spirit within you, which gives you the power to obey Him. The Ten Commandments haven't changed; they're still in effect today. God expects you to keep those laws until eternity. As you yield yourself through the Holy Spirit, you are controlled and guided by Him. You are set free to obey as you depend upon the power of the Holy Spirit working within you, and believe God will do what He promised when He said, "I will put my spirit within you, and cause you to walk in my statutes" (Ezekiel 36:27, KJV).

As you continue to yield yourself to the Holy Spirit, you will not obey the desires and lust of your flesh, and you will no longer be in bondage to the law. Now, for those of you who don't know what the law was, it was law without the Holy Spirit living inside of you. In the Old Testament there were 613 laws that kept people in condemnation because they didn't have anything to help them escape the consequences from disobeying God's laws. He realized man wasn't able to obey Him without His spirit.

God thought He could trust His Angels to obey His laws, but that turned out to be a fatal disappointment. He sent two hundred Angels to Mount Hermon to teach the people the ways of God, and they failed Him. They started teaching men and women how to make weapons for warfare. They taught them how to do all kinds of magic and sorcery. They taught the people every evil imaginable. They were beside themselves when the people started worshiping them as gods. The Angels held a meeting and made an oath to marry mortal women to have offspring in the earth realm. They didn't realize the off-spring they produced were going to become giants. They were half-human and half-Angelic. They wanted to reproduce themselves in the earth realm. God couldn't even trust His Angels to turn the hearts of the people back to God. Once the Angels failed their mission, God knew He had to come Himself. He sent Jesus, who had His spirit in Him to get the job done. Can God trust and count on you to turn men's hearts back to him?

Christians who yield themselves to the lust of their flesh are led and motivated by fleshly desires and are condemned.

They are rebelling and stand guilty before God. But "There is no condemnation to them which are in Christ Jesus, who walk not after the flesh, but after the spirit" (Romans 8:1, KJV).

God understands the difficult challenges you face walking between two worlds—the natural world and the spiritual world. In the natural world, your thoughts, which involve your imagination, attitudes, preconceived ideas, circumstances, emotions, speech, hearing, and vision, influence you. It's the part of you that's dominated by old habits and by the power of sin.

In the spirit world, God expects His people to live in a rhythm of miracles, free from the bondage of sin and death. The spiritual man is the part of you that is redeemed by the Blood of the Lamb, saved by grace, and freed from the consequences of sin and death. When your flesh dies, you live on eternally in the spirit world.

The Meaning of Our Father's Prayer

Our Father in Heaven, hallowed be thy name: This indicates you have direct access to the Father. You don't need to go through anyone to get to Him. Jesus' suffering gave you legal bonding entrance to the Father in His name. You don't need a priest or a preacher to gain access to Him. However, you do need them to teach you God's word.

Thy kingdom come, thy will be done in earth, as it is in Heaven: When you pray, you bring Heaven to earth. You are giving the Father complete access into your life. His will for you in Heaven will manifest and be done on earth through you. Allow the Holy Spirit to guide you daily. Reject self-will. Trust God in every area of your life. Include and put God first in everything you do.

Give us this day our daily bread: This gives you daily instructions to continue to walk in obedience to the Father's will. Jesus spent time in prayer daily, receiving instructions from the Father, which is also the Holy Spirit living in you to guide and keep you from temptation, hurt, harm, and danger.

And forgive us our debts, as we forgive our debtors: If you have any un-forgiveness in you, let it go! Dismiss bitterness, hatred, animosity, grudges, prejudice, and anything you are holding against someone. Forgive and release them. If anyone owes you anything, forgive them and charge it to Jesus. Forgiveness is an open door to your breakthroughs and blessings that are coming your way.

And lead us not into temptation but deliver us from evil: For Thine is the kingdom, and the power, and the glory, forever, amen: You're asking God to help you deny fleshly and earthly desires that bring you into temptation and sin. It was Eve's desire for more knowledge than God allotted her that brought sin into the world. Be aware of your fleshly and earthly desires. If you follow the Holy Spirit that's in you, there will be no time to yield to temptation when it's presented to you. Ask the Holy Spirit to protect you from evil that has the appearance of looking good. The Father will heal you everywhere you hurt. Ask for His help in times of trials and testing. Don't seek things. Look for God, and the things you need of this world will be added and given to you by God the Father.

Bible Verses to Quote Daily
to Feel the Presence of God

God will keep you in perfect peace, those whose mind are stayed on thee. **Isaiah 26:3, KJV**

Cast all your cares on the Lord for He cares for you: **1 Peter 5:7, KJV**

If God be for you who can be against you: **Romans 8:31, KJV**

The thief come to kill, steal, and destroy, but come that you might have life, and have it more abundantly: **John10:10, KJV**

This is the day that the Lord has made let's rejoice and be glad in it: **Psalm 118:24, KJV**

I can do all things through Christ that strengthens me: **Philippians 4:13,KJV**

Fear not; for I am with thee be not dismayed; for I am thy God; I will strengthen thee; yea, I will help thee yea, I will uphold thee with my right hand: **Isaiah 41:10, KJV**

Without faith it is impossible to please God, for whoever would draw near to God must believe that He exists and that He rewards those that seek Him. **Hebrews: 11:6, KJV**

Delight yourself in the Lord and He will give you the desires of your heart: **Psalm 37:4, KJV**

Taste and see that the Lord is good; blessed is the one who takes refuge in Him. **Psalm 34:8, KJV**

Come unto me, all ye that labor and are heavy burden, and I will give you rest: **Matthew 11:28, KJV**

Stand still and know that I'm God; Great is the Lord: He is worthy to be praised I will exalt His name forever more: **Psalm 46:10, KJV**

Trust in the Lord with all thine heart; and lean not unto thine own understanding. In all thy ways acknowledge him, and he shall direct thy paths. **Proverbs 3:5-6, KJV**

God is faithful, He will not suffer you to be tempted above what ye are able to bear. But will with the temptation also make a way to escape, that ye may be able to bear it. **1 Corinthians 10:13, KJV**

Those who hope in the Lord will renew their strength. They shall mount up with wings as eagles; they shall run and not get weary; they shall walk and not faint. **Isaiah 40:31**

Whatsoever you do, do it heartily, as to the Lord, and not unto men **Colossians 3:23, KJV**

We know all things work together for good to them that love God, to them that are called according to His purpose: **Romans 8:28, KJV**

Weeping may endure for a night, but joy cometh in the morning: **Psalm 30:5 KJV**

One thing I have desired of the Lord, that I will seek after, that I may dwell in the house of the Lord all the days of my life. **Psalm 27:4, KJV**

A new commandment that I give to you, that ye love one another: just as I have loved you: **John 13:34-35, KJV**

The Lord our God is one God, and thou shalt love the Lord thy God with all thy heart and with all thy soul, and with all your mind, and with all thy strength: this is the first commandment **Mark 12:29-30, KJV**

But you are a chosen people, royal priesthood, a holy nation, God's special possession, that you may declare the praises of him who called you out of darkness into His marvelous light: **1Peter 2:9, KJV**

Therefore, if anyone is in Christ, he is a new creature; old things are passed away; behold, all things are made new: **2 Corinthians 5:17, KJV**

For there is now no condemnation to them which are in Christ Jesus, who walk not after the flesh, but after the spirit, **Romans 8:1, KJV**

Nor height, nor depth, or any other creature, shall be able to separate us from the love of God, which is in Christ Jesus our Lord. **Romans 8:39, KJV**

For God so loved the world, that he gave his only begotten son, that whosoever believe in him should not perish, but have everlasting life: **John 3:16, KJV**

Let your light shine before men, that they may see your good works, and glorify your Father which is in heaven: **Matthew: 5:16, KJV**

By this shall all men know ye are my disciples, if ye have love one to another: **John 13:35, KJV**

Until now you have asked nothing in my name. Ask, and you will receive, that your joy may be full: **John 16:24**

But seek ye first the kingdom of God, and his righteousness; and all these things shall be added unto you. **Matthew 6:33**

For God sent not his son in the world to condemn the world, but that the world through him might be saved: **John 3:17**

If thou confess with thy mouth the Lord Jesus, and shall believe in thine heart that God hath raised him from the dead, thou shalt be saved: **Romans 10:9**

I'm the way, the truth, and the light. No man cometh to the Father except by me: **John 14:6**

Thoughts to Remember

Thoughts to Remember

Thoughts to Remember